MINNESOTA II

MINNESOTA II

PHOTOGRAPHY BY RICHARD HAMILTON SMITH
TEXT BY RICHARD A. COFFEY

GRAPHIC ARTS CENTER PUBLISHING COMPANY
PORTLAND, OREGON

International Standard Book Number 0-912856-87-4
Library of Congress Catalog Card Number 84-80124
Copyright ©1984 by Graphic Arts Center Publishing Company
P.O. Box 10306 • Portland, Oregon 97210 • 503/226-2402
Designer • Robert Reynolds
Typographer • Paul O. Giesey/Adcrafters
Printer • Graphic Arts Center
Bindery • Lincoln & Allen
Printed in the United States of America

To my parents, Phil and Toni
for teaching the pursuit of excellence.
To Earl for the first camera.
To JB for her understanding and love.

Richard Hamilton Smith

Page 2: North arm of Burntside Lake in northeastern Minnesota near the Boundary Waters Canoe Area. It is estimated that there are about fifteen thousand lakes and twenty-five thousand miles of rivers and streams in the state. Each year more than a half million boaters use Minnesota's waterways to fish and sail, to waterski and canoe, and to relax in the quiet of open water.

Right: A northern Minnesota farm near Park Rapids in Hubbard County. Twenty-three million acres, or half of Minnesota's land area, is cropland. The state is first in United States production of wild rice, sugar beets, and timothy seed.

Left: The three hundred-year-old "Witch Tree" grows in a rock crevice overlooking Lake Superior near Grand Portage in northeastern Minnesota. Believing it possessed by evil spirits, early visitors left gifts of tobacco at the base of the tree to ensure their safe passage through the treacherous waters of Superior. *Below:* Entrance to Minnesota's seaport at Duluth, twenty-three hundred miles from the Atlantic Ocean.

Below: The capital of Minnesota, Saint Paul is an elegant blend of history and contemporary enterprise. Selected as the site of Minnesota's World Trade Center in 1983, the city took its name from a log cabin chapel dedicated to Saint Paul, the apostle of nations, in 1841. *Right:* The Saint Louis River Gorge in Jay Cooke State Park, northeastern Minnesota. The River once drained Glacial Lake Upham, carving the Park's picturesque dalles, which are visited by thousands of tourists.

Left: A southwestern Minnesota corn field near Marshall in Lyons County, the heart of premium agricultural land and a national leader in food processing. *Below:* Spring melt on Leech Lake, Cass County, Minnesota. Many state residents gauge the arrival of spring by the breakup of ice on the larger lakes. The Leech Lake "ice-out" occurs in late April or early May. *Overleaf:* Canoeists paddle noiselessly in the Boundary Waters Canoe Area. Recreational use of Minnesota's wilderness, increasing sharply after World War II, created conflicts between conservationists and developers over mining, logging, and motorized access to the remote, pristine areas.

Below: Minnesota's principal resource: her people. Although the first Europeans in the state were French explorers, traders, and trappers, the first permanent settlers were New England Yankees followed by German and Scandinavian immigrants. Today, more than four million people live in the state—nearly half in the Twin Cities area. *Right:* A fox squirrel raids a southeastern Minnesota corn crib. *Overleaf:* A freighter passes a Duluth lighthouse. Ships from thirty-five foreign nations visit Minnesota's seaport via the Saint Lawrence Seaway, and they are joined by several thousand lake freighters operated by Canadian and American firms.

ON NEAR SHORES

A loud bell rings and a deep steam horn bellows, wiping away the screams of the gulls, the shouts of the tourists, and the crashing of the waves on the stony beach of Duluth's Minnesota Point. The crowd moves rapidly toward the canal and I, moving with them, hide my hamburger from a suspicious gull who waddles after me. The loud bell has halted automobile traffic. The aerial lift bridge, which spans a 300-foot wide canal connecting Duluth's harbor with Lake Superior, begins its ascent.

"It rises 120 feet in fifty-five seconds", a woman shouts to her husband as she reads from a brochure. The ship waiting passage acknowledges the rising bridge with another blast of its horn and slowly starts toward us. A father hoists his son to his shoulders, as the great Greek ship *Ermis* enters the canal. A lady next to me shouts that she has a cousin in Kansas City whose name is Ermis. "She's about that big too!" the woman screams above the voice on a loudspeaker that is explaining *Ermis* is carrying a load of grain — perhaps as much as twenty-six thousand tons or nearly a million bushels. Her engines rumble and we who had come to the canal to watch the ships feel the rumble in our stomachs as *Ermis* passes us, fifty feet away.

I join the crowd walking down the pier and follow the ship's progress as she clears the canal. Family snapshots are hastily organized in front of the departing ship while several photographers in search of higher art pause over their cameras for the moment the ship gains open water. In the heart of North America, 2,300 miles from the Atlantic Ocean, *Ermis* has just departed the twelfth largest harbor in the United States, the largest harbor on the Great Lakes. As the rumble of the engines fades and the roar of the waves fills the silence, the crowd breaks up and I follow a group of visitors into the nearby Canal Park Museum.

Surrounded by artifacts of Great Lakes shipping, I learn that nearly a half million people visit the canal during the ten-month shipping season. More important, each year about two thousand ships carrying a total of forty million tons of cargo including grain, iron ore, coal, and cement products generate almost two hundred million dollars in revenue shared by the Minnesota port community of Duluth and its Wisconsin neighbor, Superior. Reading statistics about the harbor, a man looks at me and says, "You never think much about having these big boats right in Minnesota". "Ships!" his wife corrects him. "You fish from a boat, these are ships", and she points to the models of lake freighters in a display case. As I move through the Museum I realize how little I have known about Minnesota's seaport, although I have lived in the state all my life.

I pass a family who stand quietly reading about the *Edmund Fitzgerald*. Late one night in November of 1975, an ore freighter sank in Lake Superior during a violent storm. The *Edmund Fitzgerald* had gone down with all hands, and the bodies were never recovered. Lake Superior, the largest of the Great Lakes, is the largest freshwater lake in the world: 383 miles long, 160 miles wide, with an average depth of 487 feet. The Lake's western shore is Minnesota's North Shore, a hundred and fifty miles of rugged coastline running north of Duluth to the Canadian border. It was on these shores that French explorers found Indians while searching for a northwest passage to the Orient.

The Dakota and the Ojibway Indians did not enrich the French visitors with gold and spices but with fur, beaver fur. In the 1600s, Europeans with a mind and a purse for fashion wore beaver hats. When explorers in North America returned to Europe with samples of the pelt, trappers, traders, and explorers financed by England, France, and private investors rushed to the Great Lakes. Where there was fur, there was wealth, and by the mid-1600s the Great Lakes had become a principal transportation route for traders. In 1668, two French adventurers, Pierre Esprit Radisson and Medard Chouard des Groseilliers, sailed to England to propose to a group of London merchants the possibilities of fur exploration through the Hudson Bay. The Frenchmen, weary of the heavy taxes imposed by the French in Quebec, inspired the English to form the Hudson Bay Company in 1670. The pressure on the beaver population began.

Nine years after the birth of the Hudson Bay Company, and just under the windows of today's Canal Museum, another young French adventurer, Daniel Greysolan Sieur du Luth, is said to have portaged his heavy canoes across the sandbar known today as Minnesota Point. If I had been standing here three hundred years ago, it is probable that I would have glimpsed Duluth's namesake and witnessed his efforts to make peace between the Ojibway and Dakota Indians, because trading with the Indians for fur was only possible if they were at peace.

Minnesota's first great resource greatly excited France and England, and for over two hundred years there was trapping and exploration and trapping and war between the two countries, and eventually trapping and settlement until there was nary a beaver to be found. By 1840, the beaver in Minnesota was nearly extinct. Traders, however, did a brisk business in pelts of fisher and mink, wolf, raccoon and bear. It appeared that the fur trade could go on forever; traders, investors, and consumers believed that the resource was unlimited.

The workers of the fur trade were the voyageurs, the "travelers". These hardy French Canadians hauled the goods to be traded across the Great Lakes in spring and hauled out the fur in the fall. The voyageurs were expert sailors, guiding their forty-foot birchbark canoes along the coastland of the stormy lakes, across rugged portages, and through mosquito-infested swamplands that led inland to the fur. The voyageurs from the interior met the voyageurs of the Great Lakes at Grand Portage, the headquarters of the North West Company, on the northeastern tip of Minnesota, and perhaps it was there that a visitor would have heard the songs of these canoemen, these travelers who had journeyed the northern boundary lakes and streams of Minnesota and the Great Lakes east to Montreal. Fur trading was dangerous work on dangerous waters, and it was the work of the voyageurs for more than two hundred and fifty years. Today, shipping on the Great Lakes is the work of *Ermis* and her crew and the crews and ships that fly the flags of many nations.

A light rain begins to fall in the park below the Museum and tourists abandon picnics and head for their cars. From the Museum's windows Lake Superior appears gray as stone, as gray as the sky. Where they meet there lies a veil of white haze. *Ermis* is gone, steaming toward the locks at Sault Sainte Marie, twenty-eight hours away. Without the locks at "The Soo", and the locks and channels below Lake Huron that are part of the Saint Lawrence Seaway System, Duluth might be a regional harbor, isolated from the national and world markets which it serves today. It was in 1855 that the first lock was built at Sault Sainte Marie, overcoming the Saint Mary's River rapids and permitting large wooden ships access to Duluth and Superior from Chicago and Cleveland. There was a land rush of sorts, on the southwestern shores of Lake Superior, but settlement occurred in the town of Superior. Duluth had a problem: Minnesota Point, the ten-mile-long sandbar, created a natural harbor for Superior, but it created a hazardous approach to Duluth. An early visitor to the region, Dr. William Worrall Mayo, who would later establish a medical practice in southern Minnesota at Rochester, found Superior in the 1850s a rough and tumble town with a few stores and boarding houses and a newspaper. What he saw of Duluth, cut off from Lake traffic, was a shanty town.

The rain stops, and breaks appear in the heavy overcast. A young woman is leading a very old man through the Museum. She is reading the labels to him and watching his eyes to see that he has heard. His eyes are expressionless, but when he looks out over the harbor, he smiles. She lets him pause at the window and remember; perhaps it was a very long time ago. A new shift of visitors arrives on the canal to await the passage of another freighter.

It is growing late and I take a short walk through the streets of downtown Duluth, a lakeside city of ninety-five thousand people which stretches twenty-three miles along Lake Superior's southwestern shore. Only a few miles wide, the city lies on the shoreland beneath a ridge that rises sharply on the west. As I dash across an intersection during the evening rush hour, I notice that the setting sun already casts long shadows in the city beneath the hill. The orange light spreads a warm glow across the rich mixture of late nineteenth century commercial architecture and contemporary glass and steel structures which give Minnesota's third largest city a feeling both of deep roots and scars. Duluth's prosperity has risen and fallen with world demand for the iron ore, grain, coal, and taconite which she ships through her port.

While Superior, Wisconsin grew during the 1850s, Duluth remained a muddy hillside of shantys. But when the banks failed in 1857, and Superior lost population and businesses, Duluth remained — a ghost town can survive anything. In 1866 the Philadelphia financier Jay Cooke toured the harbor and became convinced that Duluth could become "the Chicago at the head of the Lakes". Four years later, Cooke and several Philadelphia banks completed a railroad from Saint Paul. While the railroad was under construction, Cooke built cargo docks, a bank, and a church, and purchased seven thousand town lots. He built grain elevators and convinced Northern Pacific Railroad to invest a half million dollars for the construction of steel mills. The potential of Minnesota's iron ore had become clear.

In the spring of 1871 the people of Duluth dug a canal across Minnesota Point and created access to the harbor. This proved their insurance when, during the panic of 1873, Jay Cooke's empire collapsed. Although the population of six thousand declined to a little over a thousand after the panic of 1874, ships began to enter Duluth Bay. As grains from the prairies of western Minnesota arrived, elevators were built, and, with the growth of midwestern cities which created a tremendous demand for lumber, northern Minnesota forests supplied Duluth's saw mills.

Bust became boom, and by 1887 Duluth had thirty thousand people, saw and planing mills, grain elevators, wholesale houses, iron companies, publishing houses, breweries, and a bottling works. Duluth mills cut thirty-five million board feet of lumber in 1880 and one hundred and sixty million board feet in 1885. Duluth received half a million bushels of wheat in 1880 and nearly fifteen million by 1885. The city was propelled through the end of the nineteenth century by America's demand for lumber and wheat and by something new that Duluth could load on the ships which sailed the Great Lakes: Minnesota iron ore.

I watch as the light of day fades and sailboats drift quietly in a

Left to right: Loading iron ore at the Hanna Mine Company in northern Minnesota. ■ A yard at Burlington Northern. ■ Professional football: the Minnesota Vikings. ■ Cross-country skier glides through east-central Minnesota. ■

fair breeze. The sharp, white sails pierce the blue black lake and sky. Now a freighter emerges from the canal, and the sailboats quickly give chase like chicks in pursuit of the broody hen. They follow the ship into the night, and the street lights of Duluth sparkle on the dark water.

In May of 1959, the British vessel, *Ramon De Larrinaga,* arrived in Duluth to carry a load of grain back through the Saint Lawrence Seaway — a joint project between Canada and the United States which opened the Great Lakes to the Atlantic Ocean. The Minnesota port became a world port, and the fortunes of Duluth came to depend upon world-wide demand. Much of Minnesota's history began on the North Shore; much of Minnesota's resources — fur, white pine, iron ore, and wheat — left by way of Lake Superior.

There is a night song of the channel buoys, and a glow of ships' lights on the horizon. There is a roar of activity in the harbor and quiet in the city, a long necklace of twinkling lights beneath the ridge. In the morning I will drive up that hill to the airport where I will continue my travels into Minnesota.

AN AERIAL PERSPECTIVE

At the airport, on the hill eight hundred feet above Duluth, I turn in my car and walk out to my rented airplane. There is a gentle northwest wind and the small Cessna rocks in the breeze like a small boat moored in a waking harbor. I check the oil and the fuel supply and go into the flight office to take a look at the weather forecast. High pressure is sprawled out over the Dakotas. I could not ask for better weather, especially after weeks of rain.

Minnesotans are impressed by their weather and they are forever talking about it and trying to outguess the weather services. Homespun weather reporting relies on arthritic knees as much as it relies on wind direction and cloud formation. A man will cover his woodpile on a clear bright day if his knee aches — throwing on the tarp with as much determination as if it were raining.

Minnesota's climate is composed of four seasons, each with a distinct weather pattern and each lasting about three months. Summer begins in June when low pressure west of Minnesota and high pressure to the east permit a flow of warm, moist air up from the Gulf of Mexico. Moisture and unstable air make June the month of violent thunderstorms and tornadoes which parade across the state from the west. In July and August the air is more stable, a predominant high pressure clears the skies, and the state heats up. A week in the high Fahrenheit nineties is not unusual, and Minnesotans live on their patios, on the beaches, and in their boats, fishing away the long summer days.

Fall often visits one night late in August when one wears a sweater on the porch and prefers a cup of hot coffee over a glass of iced tea. But fall arrives toward the end of September when the leaves lose their chlorophyll and reveal their true colors of orange and red and yellow. The air of fall is cool and dry for the most part, but it is the time of the year when Minnesotans begin thinking about winter.

Winter preoccupies the Minnesotan. Although the meteorological winter begins in December, a sleetstorm in November sends residents scurrying to their service stations to get their automobiles dressed in lightweight oil, new tires, and batteries. December is pictorial. The days are short, the nights are long, and in homes all over the state lights blaze as festive parties celebrate any cause: the first snow, a new pair of cross-country skis, the end of the year, anything to bring friends together out of the darkness into warm light. It is January and February which have given Minnesota a reputation for being a cold and inhospitable place to live.

But Minnesota is not inhospitable. The temperature may drop twenty or thirty degrees below zero on occasion, the wind may take your breath on occasion, snowstorms will close schools and stop traffic, but Minnesotans love winter and snow. They ski on the snow and they snowmobile through it; resident runners jog through drifts, and early morning commuters crawl down glazed freeways on their way to work. On a clear and snappy January day, when the temperature climbs to five below zero after a week of cold weather, fishermen will drive to their favorite lake, drill a hole through the ice, set up a comfortable chair, and while away a refreshing afternoon fishing. On a very cold day it may take a half hour to get dressed to go outside for fifteen minutes. It may take an hour to start the car only to move it around the block so a snowplow can clean the street. Winter storms can be dangerous too. Unwary travelers have been caught unprepared and stalled along roads in sub-zero weather. One soon learns that winter has the winning hand and that the weather must be taken into account when considering plans for travel.

One also learns that spring eventually will come. The snow will melt, the ice will thaw, windows will be opened, garages will be swept, automobiles washed, and sweaters packed away for another six months.

I dig out my maps for the short flight to Minneapolis — 140 miles away, a little over an hour's flight in the Cessna. I return to the airplane with the good feeling that comes with an early morning flight — a smooth and restful way to begin a day of business in the

Twin Cities. I start the engine and go through the checklist before I call up ground control for taxi instructions to the active runway. As I receive clearance and begin to move across the ramp I hear the thunder of a jet engine. Looking out my window I watch an Air National Guard F4 climb into the morning sky.

Cleared by the tower to take off, I push the throttle forward and begin to roll. A little back pressure on the control wheel and the Cessna fairly jumps into the calm air. As the runway and the airport terminal fall away beneath me, I turn south to a course that will take me over the Saint Louis River. I bid the tower good day and climb to two thousand feet, high enough not to be a noise problem for anyone trying to enjoy a quiet morning and low enough to see something of northeastern Minnesota. I reduce the engine power to cruise and trim the airplane to maintain altitude, then I settle back to enjoy a doughnut and a cup of steaming black coffee from my thermos.

Lake Superior appears as a great white sheet out my left window. Below me the Saint Louis River snakes through the Jay Cooke State Park, a spectacular rock gorge two miles west of Duluth where thousands of visitors go to camp, hike, and fish, and to photograph the columbine, rock fern, and bluebells which grow along the rock outcropping. Some canoe the Saint Louis River and make the same portages that the adventurer du Luth made in 1679 when he explored inland waterways.

I am flying south, a few miles west of the Wisconsin and Minnesota border. The radio crackles with the voice of a pilot making an approach to the Duluth airport. Behind me, about one hundred and thirty miles north, lies the vast wild land of Minnesota's border with Canada. The Boundary Waters Canoe Area, a part of the National Wilderness Preservation System, is a million acres of protected wilderness with almost two hundred thousand acres of lakes and short streams. Today, canoeists paddle across lakes which have barely changed since the voyageurs paddled there two hundred years ago. Two hundred and fifty miles to my right and north a few degrees, across the state's central lake district to the prairies of the northwest lies Minnesota's border with North Dakota and the Red River Valley.

Minnesota is a land of rivers and lakes and streams. There are twenty-five thousand miles of rivers and streams; no one has finished counting the lakes. The state license plate declares Minnesota is the *Land of 10,000 Lakes,* but that is about five thousand too few for most experts, who agree that approximately three million acres of water lie within the state's borders. Water in Minnesota flows in three directions along a ridge, northwest of

Duluth, which is a hundred miles wide east to west. Water on the north slope of the ridge flows to the Canadian border and on to Hudson Bay. Water on the south slope drains into Lake Superior. On the west, water travels to the Mississippi River, which originates in northwestern Minnesota, in Lake Itasca, and journeys more than two thousand miles south to the Gulf of Mexico.

Glaciers carved the face of Minnesota, glaciers and ten thousand years of roaring currents which hewed deep gorges in the granite of northern Minnesota and cut river valleys in the limestone and sandstone of the south. The ice sheets, which covered all but the southeastern corner of the state, melted at the end of the Pleistocene Age and deposited rock, sand, and clay. The melting created gigantic lakes, and these, draining at different rates, gave rise to the streams which would become the rivers and the basins which would become the lakes. Great chunks of ice melted slowly, creating deep cold lakes, and smaller chunks created numerous kettles and potholes. Both Minnesota's topographic character and its resources result from the glaciers' meltdown.

The greatest of the glacial lakes was Agassiz. Named for a Swiss-American geologist, Louis Agassiz, the lake probably covered about eighty thousand square miles; seventeen thousand acres covered northwestern Minnesota. For thousands of years, the water drained, depositing rich sediment and creating a flat lake bed many hundreds of feet thick. Today, the traveler in northwestern Minnesota knows he has reached the western plains: the land is flat, broad, and spectacular.

Below me, a red-tailed hawk is circling in an early morning thermal. The sun catches his bright colors, and as he passes behind me I am tempted to close the throttle and follow the bird in his graceful spiral over the forest canopy. The hawk migration has begun, and I think of the place a mile east of Duluth where hundreds of people come in September to watch the passage of thousands of hawks. On a clear day, when the wind blows hard from the west, hawks coming south from northern Minnesota, Canada, and the Arctic hug the northern shore to avoid a long flight over the open waters of Lake Superior. At a place called Hawk Ridge, birders wearing warm jackets observe many species of hawk, including the peregrine falcon and the gyrfalcon and have counted over thirty thousand broad-winged hawks in their annual passage.

Below me, the ninety thousand-acre Nemadji State Forest spreads its broad green mantle far into the morning haze. It is a wild and unsettled place, the Nemadji, a forest of aspen and birch, spruce, and balsam fir. Here and there a white pine pokes up through the hardwood canopy, but for the most part the great pine are gone. White pine was Minnesota's second industry, and it brought wealth to a few people and work to many immigrants who settled the land.

But the white pine story did not begin in Minnesota. Europeans met the tree on the North Atlantic seaboard, where it was harvested for the masts of ships and for its lumber, which was lightweight, strong, and easy to work. The white pine grew tall and straight, and to the man on the forest floor, it seemed the forests of pine went on forever. For two centuries, Maine was the leading lumber center. After New York and Pennsylvania, they logged the white pine of Michigan and Wisconsin, and by the early 1840s the lumbermen had come to Minnesota. The Yankee timber cruisers were impressed by Minnesota's white pine. They saw trees two hundred feet tall and five feet in diameter and forests "as far as the eye could reach."

I turn the airplane to the right ten degrees and pull back on the throttle to lose some altitude. Below me a deserted farmstead lies deep in a thicket of hazel brush surrounded by a forest of aspen. The weathered wood is silver white in the bright sunlight, and the roof is torn by years of wind and rain and wet, heavy snows. I guide the Cessna in a low, tight turn around the farm. Two crows fly up from the rear of an outbuilding. The north country is sprinkled with the remains of farms abandoned after the promises of turn-of-the-century land agents failed to materialize.

It was cheap land when the pine was all gone, and a man who had rented the rich soil of southern Minnesota and Iowa saw his chance to buy his own place for a few dollars an acre. Ninety-day corn grows comfortably within the one hundred and thirty-day growing season of southern Minnesota, but a man can fail when he plants ninety-day corn in a latitude where the growing season is ninety days. The soil of southern Minnesota is rich and deep under a mat of prairie grass. In northern Minnesota, the soil is shallow and laced with thick roots and stones. A man couldn't plow the acid soil until he pulled the giant stumps and cleared the brush the loggers left.

I push the throttle forward and climb into the sun. I turn south and look for a cash-crop farm. I see none. There is pastureland. I see hay and a dairy herd. To the west it appears someone is cutting pulpwood, but the pine was the principal resource and it is gone.

The white pine in Minnesota stood on Indian land until the treaties of 1837 when the Ojibway and the Dakota signed over to the government what may have been the richest pinery on the continent. It was a triangle of timberlands extending from the Mississippi River east to the Saint Croix, north to the Nemadji, and south to the land which is now the cities of Minneapolis and Saint Paul. They say the ink was still wet on the treaties when the first white pine fell. And when the white pine fell, they choked the streams and rivers and filled the log booms at the sawmills on the Mississippi and Saint Croix Rivers. In twenty years, from 1854 to 1874, 3.5 billion feet of timber passed through the Saint Croix boom alone.

The end came fast. In 1890, a half billion board feet of lumber passed through the Saint Croix mills. By 1914, the white pine of the Saint Croix Delta was gone. The land was stripped and the forest floor littered with the refuse of logging. Communities inland along the railroads lived in fear of drought. While homesteaders moved into the cut-over lands, and sawmill towns flourished, thick mats of dry branches and tree tops exploded into flame, and reports of tragic fires in Minnesota, Michigan, and Wisconsin played on the front pages of community newspapers.

Flying southwest I cross the freeway connecting the Twin Cities with Duluth. As far as I can see the land is rough and heavily wooded with aspen and birch. There are stands of tamarack on the bogs and groves of black spruce which have ventured far out into the wetlands. Here and there I spot a small, almost perfectly round lake, a glacial kettle, where thousands of years ago a single block of ice slowly melted. Rivers and streams course through the wild landscape, and trails — perhaps old logging roads — zigzag through the brush. Today they are probably used by hunters in pursuit of the ruffed grouse and woodcock, the white-tailed deer and black bear.

As I reach the halfway point between the Twin Cities and Duluth, I see large tracts of cleared land. I see pastureland, hay and corn fields, and a dairy herd. The Hinckley Chamber of Commerce refers to itself as the place "where the farm meets the forest," but the village also suffered one of the worst after shocks of the logging industry. It was Saturday, September 1, 1894. After a summer of drought and many small forest fires, burning waste ignited cutover forest south of Hinckley and, pushed by a brisk afternoon wind, became a firestorm, destroying six villages and killing more than four hundred people, almost three hundred in Hinckley alone. This disaster and others shocked Minnesotans and stirred the legislature to take steps toward conservation, fire prevention, and the regulation of logging operations.

Today, the Division of Forestry within the Minnesota Department of Natural Resources has jurisdiction over four and a half million acres of state-owned forest and assists with the fire protection of an additional twelve million acres of timber. Forest management balances the harvest of trees with the need for recreational space and the maintenance of a healthy woodland. This is part of the white pine legacy. In Hinckley, a museum which tells the story of forest fire is also part of the legacy.

As I fly south, minutes of latitude are buying days of growing season, the woodland is disappearing, and the land is becoming increasingly agricultural. The prairie soils of southern and western Minnesota are rich in nutrients, and as early as 1850 investors saw the potential of the wheat crop to be harvested from these lands. The businessmen were right: wheat put Minnesota on the map as a major, mid-continent trade center; wheat, ground into flour in the mills on the banks of the Mississippi, gave Minneapolis a world-wide reputation for grain milling and marketing.

Twenty miles north of Minneapolis and Saint Paul, I tune in approach control on my radio. The talk is brisk as flights from Chicago, Denver, and Boston mix with departures to Phoenix, Portland, and Miami. Ahead I see the Twin Cities on the horizon: glass and steel glitters under blue skies in bright sun. Here, two million people, half of the state's population, live and work in a seven-county metropolitan area. Here lies the heart of Minnesota, the center of trade and finance, industry and art, higher education and state government. Here, on the banks of the Mississippi, Minnesota, and Saint Croix rivers, where the beaver's fur was traded, the pine milled, and the wheat ground into flour, is the center of the state's transportation system. Roads and rail radiate from the Twin Cities, commercial river traffic churns north and south along the Mississippi, while the busy metropolitan airports service flights from around the world and light aircraft from any of the 140 Minnesota airports.

Below, I see chains of suburban homes snaking around small lakes and hiding deep beneath canopies of oak and maple trees. A large home on my left has sprouted a long white fence which encloses a barn and harbors riding horses. Roadways twist and turn, following small lakes, and empty into wide ribbons of freeway which are flanked by trailer courts, shopping centers, and car lots with fluttering pennants.

Approach control gives me a turn to the southwest and permission to enter the busy Terminal Control Area. I reduce the power a few RPMs and make another turn for the controller. I check my instruments and watch for aircraft traffic. Far above me a Northwest Airlines 747 climbs over the western suburbs. Northwest is a homegrown air carrier which was born in Saint Paul in 1926 and is today one of the healthiest airlines in the country.

The morning rush hour is over, but the freeways which circle the Twin Cities are busy; shopping center parking lots are filling up. I contact the control tower at Crystal Airport, one of seven satellite airports in the metropolitan area which relieves the pressure of general aviation traffic from Minneapolis-Saint Paul International Airport. The tower clears me to the airport traffic pattern and I continue my descent, noticing that the wooded yards of the city below are salted by brightly colored leaves but that the peak of fall color is a few weeks away. Cleared for a landing, I reduce the power and drop a few degrees of flaps. Then I am rushing over the tops of trees and roofs and a lake. There is a sailboat on the lake. Another notch of flaps, a blur of trees, and now 3,250 feet of asphalt in front of me. I touch down lightly with a squeak and turn off the runway to call ground control for clearance to the ramp. Airplanes are moving at the flight schools on the field, and a Piper twin is off-loading three businessmen dressed in tan trench coats.

Minnesota has about seventeen thousand active pilots, flying about six thousand general aviation aircraft. Some of us use airplanes for business, some fly north to a wilderness lake for a weekend fishing trip, others pack the family into an airplane for a Thanksgiving visit to grandma's house. All of us know that Minnesota was the boyhood home of Charles Lindbergh, who grew up in Little Falls, ninety miles northwest of the Twin Cities, and was an airmail pilot before he flew his 33½-hour, non-stop flight from New York to Paris in the *Spirit of St. Louis,* May 21, 1927.

I shut down the engine, and as the whining sound of the gyros fades, the sound of the busy city fills the cockpit. I gather my maps and bags and look up to see my wife, Jeanne, smiling through the plane's window. Four years before, we moved from the Cities to a cabin in the woods of east-central Minnesota to spend some time alone, together, away from the hustle of the city. We loved the solitude for a year and then we began to make trips "into town", back to the Twin Cities, on the pretense of having to pick up supplies. In truth, we missed what the city offered: summer concerts on the shores of a city lake; a play at the Guthrie Theater, the bookshop's warmth on cold Saturday mornings in winter. We began to visit the city as one would visit an old schoolteacher, remembering the comfort and the instructive times when the relationship made sense.

We mix with the suburban traffic as we leave the airport parking lot and head for downtown Minneapolis. "Look!" Jeanne says, pointing to a jogger flanked by two Great Danes. I watch the older man run with his dogs through the trees bordering a suburban lake. A hundred feet behind him morning traffic rushes through an

Left to right: Minnesota's state bird, the loon. ■ Voyageurs' celebration, Pine City. ■ Whitewater canoeist runs rapids in Pine County. ■ State highschool hockey tournament. ■

intersection, yet he was with his dogs as if he were on a long, lonely country road.

THE TWIN CITIAN

Driving in Minneapolis and Saint Paul and their suburbs is like driving through an enormous park. Everywhere trees tower above old homes and new. Elm, oak, maple, and spruce mix with cottonwood and pine, ash and willow. Block after block of forest live in the city and on the shores of more than twenty-five lakes within the Twin Cities' limits. There are over eight hundred lakes in the seven-county metropolitan area. This is one reason that Twin Citians behave as if they lived in a park. An attached garage may be used for the family car, but the car is parked carefully to avoid hitting the family fishing boat or sailing craft or canoe. A garage in the Twin Cities is a museum of recreational artifacts ranging from a pair of grandfather's snowshoes and a spectrum of fishing paraphernalia to a hang glider or moto-cross bike. Within the metropolitan area, there are hundreds of miles of bike trails, fifty golf courses, numerous downhill skiing sites, cross-country skiing trails, places to curl and hang glide, courts to play tennis, and all outdoors to jog.

The Twin Citian likes to be outside. The sedate person likes to be sedate outside. Weather is no problem, it simply dictates what one has to dig out of the garage. If in August you fish Bass Lake from a boat, in January you put on your snowmobile suit and arm yourself with an ice auger. Bike trails become ski trails, swimming holes become ice rinks, and decks, hooked to the back of houses, fill with several cords of seasoned oak for the woodstove or the fireplace. On a winter's night in the Twin Cities, when the snow is falling fast, and the children have come in from playing fox and goose in the backyard, you don a light parka, step outside, and listen to the snow fall. Above you drifts the smell of woodsmoke.

In the solitude of a suburban street, we turn right at a quiet corner to pass through the neighborhood where Jeanne grew up. Built during the late 1940s and early 1950s when the urban core was old and crowded, the suburbs offered large lots and low density and fresh air. The suburban ranch house with its large picture window and attached garage was a dramatic shift away from the cramped, two-story family residence of the inner city, and Twin Citians fell for it heads over their Scandinavian heels.

In 1950, the census reported a half million people living in the city of Minneapolis. Today the population is closer to 370,000. The magic of the suburbs is still strong, but the young are fascinated with the high-rise, condo life-style of the center city. On our right we see a large, three-story frame house being restored. It may have been the farmhouse which commanded the pastureland. Thirty years ago we would be driving over a rolling, treeless field upsetting dairy cows. Today the suburb is mature, and the ranch house is up to its eaves in Russian olive and honeysuckle.

Squarely pinned to the fabric of each suburb are the churches and schools and shopping centers which followed the exodus from the inner city. Each of the sixty suburban areas is well equipped to handle police, fire, and other public services and to provide quick access to hospitals. Each suburb maintains schools within one of the forty-nine school districts in the metropolitan area, and bus transportation extends to the inner city.

But it is the large stone churches and the long, flat schools, flanked by huge parking lots, which reflect the suburban philosophy of space in the 1960s; everything sprawls. The two and three-car garages attest to the need for an automobile to journey to schools, churches, workplaces, and stores. One shopping center may have been responsible for a great deal of suburban growth. Southdale, the nation's first fully enclosed, all-climate, shopping mall took root in a corn field southwest of Minneapolis during the mid-1950s. Its success led to the birth of seven additional super-malls in the Twin Cities area, and its concept was copied nationally. Minnesotans, who take some pride in their image as hardy outdoorsmen and women, flocked to the suburban shopping centers where they could buy a set of snow tires, drop off a roll of film for processing, and buy a pair of shoes and a pet turtle all under a single roof, during a blizzard.

Minneapolis and Saint Paul, which were still losing population — and shoppers — in the 1970s, began programs of renewal to bring consumers and residents back. The cities built parking ramps and skyscraping shopping centers. They built condominiums and restored run-down buildings. Former skid-rows became elegant town homes, nineteenth century warehouses became fashionable restaurants and boutiques. The Metropolitan Stadium, the Twin Cities sports arena and home of the Minnesota Vikings and the Minnesota Twins, was moved from the suburbs to an all-weather domed stadium in downtown Minneapolis. The Dome, formally named the Hubert H. Humphrey Stadium, was a shock to many football and baseball fans who counted on the weather to provide atmosphere for a game. The sun, the hot, blazing, baking July sun, seemed to some fans as much a part of baseball as the ball that went over the fence. There were football fans who would not bother to show up unless they could wear blankets and carry a thermos and brush a couple inches of snow

off their laps before they went home after a game. Nevertheless, the Dome rose, and the fans have come to the games.

About six hundred million dollars worth of private construction has blossomed around Minneapolis since the early 1970s, and to Jeanne and me it seemed that every time we came to town another tall, broad, skyscraper had been built, changing forever the way the sun would shine on the streets below. The view from my dentist's window began as a pleasant skyscape, in which fluffy cumulus clouds passed by during Novocain dreams, but slowly filled with angular dark steel and pneumatic hammering. Today my view of the sky is a reflection in the glass across the street and I, like most Twin Citians, take the change in our urban landscape as easily as we have taken to November football games in our shirt-sleeves. The downtown, dying in the 1950s, has been brought back to life by private sector money during a time when many cities discovered that the well of public money had gone dry.

We enter downtown Minneapolis on a swift, one-way throughfare and are whisked along by the pressure of noon traffic. Minneapolis people seem to accept a wide variety of contemporary architecture. Briefly skeptical, residents come to take pride in a new glass and stone development which erupts from the dust of an old, demolished building where memories were as numerous as the stones in the rubble. The fifty-seven-story IDS building shoulders above the traffic ahead of us, and City Center, opened in August of 1983, rises sixty stories across the street. The Center is home to more than ninety shops, restaurants, and services, and more than fifty are new to the downtown.

While we wait for a traffic light to change, we watch the lunch crowd fill the streets with the bright colors of designer dresses and shoes. Young girls dash across the street with their comrades in search of a quick quiche, while older professional women and men move with the casual confidence which comes from a luncheon reservation. Office workers in shirt sleeves relax on the Nicollet Mall in the sun, while visitors hug the store windows aglitter with bejeweled mannikins dressed in soft sensual leathers. A businessman in a three-piece suit reaches for a loose paper cup littering the sidewalk and chucks it into a nearby wastebasket. I think of the magazine editor who told me that he thought Minneapolis was "squeaky-clean." "Not just the streets," he said, "but politics and government and business ... life in Minneapolis is squeaky-clean; it is comfortable and predictable and secure."

Minneapolis is essentially a white-collar city, culturally attuned, socially responsible, and politically liberal. Minneapolis emerged from the nineteenth century a city of office workers engaged in food processing, grain trading, and agricultural marketing. Managers from "back east" brought with them a taste for the arts; Scandinavians infused the city with a sense for the social welfare of all citizens. These people, along with the agrarian crusaders who fought for farmers' interests, headed Minnesota down a liberal trail which has been hiked by former United States Vice-President and Senator Hubert H. Humphrey, an early architect of the Democratic Farmer Labor Party, and by rising political star Walter Mondale.

The roots of the private sector in Minneapolis and Saint Paul run deep and are often tangled in the roots of white pine and wheat. The lumber industry assembled a large work force in the state, built roads, cleared land, and, with the railroads, opened northern Minnesota to homesteaders. Some lumber kings turned to flour milling when the vast prairie lands of western Minnesota were settled by immigrants in the 1860s. The names of the lumber and wheat barons of the late nineteenth century are family names associated with the patrons of the arts in the Twin Cities today. Walker, Pillsbury, Washburn, Morrison, and Crosby are a few of the influential and prominent Minneapolis families helping to develop the Minneapolis Society of Fine Arts, which in 1983 celebrated its one hundredth anniversary.

As we leave the downtown area, we find ourselves surrounded by new high-rise residential development. It is estimated that 110,000 people work in downtown Minneapolis and that 15,000 people live there in 5,000 apartments, townhouses, and condominiums. Old hotels and warehouses have been restored to serve as future homes for a new wave of settlers who are expected to leave the suburbs for the amenities of the inner city. We pass Orchestra Hall, built in 1974 with generous donations from the private sector, which, as befits one of the country's finest orchestras, is hailed as one of the nation's greatest concert halls.

Lost in the restoration around a downtown park, we emerge on a busy street facing the Walker Art Center and the Tyrone Guthrie Theater. Thomas Walker was a lumberman with a love of art so great that in 1890 he had to hire a curator to care for his private collection. Today, the Walker Art Center is considered one of the most prestigious museums in the country. Next door, the Guthrie Theater began in the 1960s when New York director Sir Tyrone Guthrie came to Minneapolis in search of a place to practice serious theater. Guthrie's quest set the Twin Cities on the map of major American theater.

We find the Minneapolis Institute of Arts and head in to look at the Grant Wood exhibit organized by the Institute's staff. Among the paintings we find *American Gothic,* the 1930 work which depicts a staid, midwestern farmer and his daughter posed with pitchfork in front of a tidy Gothic-style farmhouse. Wood's paintings are of a Midwest which never existed: clean, rounded countryside, always bountiful, always pure in heart. But there is wit in his work which speaks of a time when the farm met face to face with the harsh realities of the industrial age.

When The Minneapolis Society of Fine Arts dedicated its first permanent building in 1915, the keynote speaker, University of Minnesota President George Vincent, said, "The Institute is our protection against provincialism, and an influence for metropolitanism." Twelve thousand visitors came the first Saturday the museum opened, and provincialism has been on the run since. Today, the Society has a yearly budget of eleven million dollars, administers the museum and the College of Art and Design, and holds a collection of sixty-five thousand objects worth over 250 million dollars. The old families and fortunes are disappearing; the legacy of the white pine, wheat, and railroads, which endowed the arts, sciences, and education in Minnesota, is fading. However, there is hope that the Midwest's great corporations will continue to support the arts and preserve the quality relationship between business and community which Minnesotans have valued for nearly a century.

Minnesota's corporate power is mighty and much of it appears in the *Fortune 500* listings. Publicly held companies such as 3M, Honeywell, General Mills, Super Valu, Dayton Hudson, Pillsbury, and International Multifoods are among the homegrown firms nurtured by entrepreneurs in the late nineteenth and early twentieth centuries.

In 1860, farmers and eighty-five flour mills produced two million bushels of wheat. In the 1890s, over five hundred flour mills processed over fifty million bushels of wheat, and Minneapolis had become the milling center of the world. From the wheat fields, the elevators, and the flour mills came the Cargill, Pillsbury, Washburn, and Peavey fortunes. In the streets beneath the mills grew the department store of George Dayton and the wholesale grocery which became Super Valu. A thermostat, invented in 1885 and marketed by a wheelbarrow manufacturer, was the foundation of Honeywell Inc. The entrepreneurial flame lit the way for Control Data, born in 1957, and the high-tech industry.

I think about the farmer as I look at the Grant Wood pictures. It was the farmer who reaped the wheat which supplied the mills which built the city. It was the railroads which charged the tariffs which nearly broke the farmers' backs. Rail transportation to the mills was an essential service to both farmer and miller, but the rates devoured the farmers' profits. The wheat grower was in trouble, until a Minnesota farmer, Oliver Kelley, organized the Patrons of Husbandry, or the Grange, in 1867 and won state regulation requiring railroads to set fixed fares and rates.

Kelley hoped to establish a social organization and an educational tool so that farmers learned from each other the business and science of agriculture, and a nationwide membership of 800,000 had certain political clout. But the farmers' troubles were not over. What the Grange could not do was solve the grasshopper problem, which began in Minnesota in 1873. When the 'hoppers showed up on a summer's wind in June, they ate nearly everything in southwestern Minnesota. An acre of land which had produced twenty-two bushels of wheat before the arrival of the grasshoppers yielded just six bushels. The state legislature voted loan money for new seed, but the insects returned, and farms failed.

By 1877 the grasshoppers had gone, but wheat rust attacked crops. More farms failed. Worst of all, one-crop farming, the planting of a single crop on the same soil year after year, was robbing the land of nutrients and reducing yield. Granger laws forced private corporations serving the public interest to submit to government control and saved the farmer from being victimized by man, but nature was yet to be tamed—or understood.

Outside the crowded art gallery the fresh September air smells of fall. Around us, turn-of-the-century homes which had nearly collapsed from neglect a few years before are now bright with Victorian colors and gingerbread and warmed with woodstoves. There is a sense of action in the neighborhood, a feeling of responsibility for what was left behind when people left the city for the suburbs. The residents that we see were young, perhaps in their twenties and thirties, and they had been working together as a community to live well.

If the restored neighborhoods of Minneapolis give one a comforting sense of security, the city of Saint Paul gives one the feeling of a warm bath, a terry robe, and a brandy. Saint Paul is a quieter place than its sister, Minneapolis, and in many ways it feels friendlier. It does not reach out and grab attention the way Minneapolis does. Saint Paul resembles the twin sister who never married and stays home minding the sewing.

The two cities are not identical twins. Although they crawled from the same cradle on the Mississippi and Minnesota rivers, not far from Saint Anthony Falls, they followed different paths through childhood. A Flemish friar, a captive of the Dakota Indians bound for the Mille Lacs Lake in 1680, saw and named Saint Anthony Falls for his patron saint. Father Louis Hennepin apparently enjoyed his capture and remained a happy observer of Dakota culture until his rescue by du Luth later in the summer.

One hundred and twenty-five years later, United States Army Lieutenant Zebulon Pike met with the Dakota at the junction of the Mississippi and Minnesota rivers and secured nine miles of land on either side of the Mississippi, including Saint Anthony Falls, for the promise of two thousand dollars. After a little rum and some gift-giving, the treaty was signed.

Fifteen years later, in 1820, Colonel Josiah Snelling brought troops to the river junction and began to build a fort overlooking the river valleys. Snelling's soldiers were Minnesota's first white loggers and sawyers, farmers, and flour millers. The fort was Minnesota's first outpost of United States authority, and it was from the fort that negotiations with the Dakota and Ojibway Indians opened Minnesota lands to lumbermen and homesteaders.

It was around Fort Snelling that Minneapolis and Saint Paul's early settlers built their respective villages. Guided by Colonel Snelling's Boston upbringing, the fort was the seedbed of culture in the upper Midwest. Theatricals, dancing, readings, and schooling took place around the fort, as well as a family life rich in the adventures of the frontier and the aroma of the wilderness. The Minnesota State Historical Society has restored the fort, and visitors can see living history complete with marching soldiers and gossiping officers' wives. What a visitor may not be able to imagine is how vast and empty these river valley lands were.

From the wall of the fort one must strain not to see the freeways, the industry, the International Airport, which was once wooded rolling hills, green and rich in summer, stark beyond an easterner's experience of winter. Zachary Taylor, later President of the United States, commanded Fort Snelling for a year and thought Minnesota the "most miserable and uninteresting country" on which he had ever laid eyes. If "Old Rough and Ready" found little to appreciate, a later commander, Seth Eastman, created scenic watercolors which give Minnesota schoolchildren an appreciation for the beauty of the frontier that became their state.

As we drive slowly through Saint Paul's streets around the government buildings which surround the State Capitol, I see in the city below the hill new construction pushing up through old neighborhoods. Bright sunlight is absorbed by the soft, dark stone of older buildings and sharply reflected by the new. Hard edges and soft meet in Saint Paul's downtown as new ideas find a place among old institutions. We have the feeling that Minneapolis's

maiden sister is dressing up to meet the twenty-first century. Apartments and condominiums, speciality shops, museums of art and science and history are sprinkled around town, mixing with office buildings, and parking lots bulging with the cars of mid-afternoon shoppers.

We went into the Historical Society's building and while Jeanne used the reference library to track down some information about pioneer women in our county, I browsed in the book shop. The State Historical Society was founded in 1849, the year Minnesota became a territory, at the urging of Territorial Governor Alexander Ramsey who sought preservation of newspapers, the "day books of history" and records. Ramsey, and others, had a vision of thousands of immigrants pouring into the territory and settling the wild lands. They could feel that there would be exciting news to preserve. News there was, but not much of it was good for Minnesota's first residents, the Indians.

About fifteen thousand Indians live in the Twin Cities today, and perhaps another fifteen thousand live on eleven reservations set aside for the Dakota and Ojibway. There is some appreciation for the Indian heritage and some curiosity about who the native Minnesotan really is. There are social programs for Indians, cultural programs about Indians, and in most tourist gift shops something made by Indians, or something which looks very much like something made by Indians, available. The fact is that treaty by treaty the Dakota and the Ojibway peoples were removed from their lands, away from the timber, off the prairies, and onto reservations. Lumbermen took the timber, homesteaders plowed the prairie, and traders and Indian agents took charge of the Indians. The injustices suffered by the Indians at the hands of unscrupulous agents were legion. In 1862 the bitterness and hatred felt by many Dakota for the white man exploded in a war which Minnesotans would long remember.

Leaving the Historical Society on foot, we hike down the capitol mall to the Minnesota Science Museum and its William McKnight 3M Omnitheater. One of the most advanced space theaters in the world, the McKnight's ceiling-to-floor screen surrounds the audience with spectacular images and sound. In the museum we look over an anthropology exhibit and find artifacts of the early Ojibway culture. I think of the one hundred and sixty years which have lapsed between the building of Fort Snelling and the building of an exhibit which displays the remains of a culture displaced by the white man.

Museums have a way of reminding people that the present was secured at some cost, that a culture is fragile, that survival is often

Left to right: Pulpwood harvest. ■ Southern Minnesota county fair. ■ Farmers' market. ■ Minnesota's state flower, the showy lady's-slipper. ■

a matter of adapting to change. Omnitheater's namesake, William McKnight, was, when he died in 1978, one of the state's wealthiest men. He knew something about survival, having helped to guide Minnesota Mining and Manufacturing through setback after setback in the early 1900s by adapting to changes in the marketplace. The point is underscored when Jeanne shows me a brochure advertising computer classes in the Museum: "Learn survival skills for the age of technology," it says.

As we leave Saint Paul we drive by the World Theater where writer and humorist Garrison Keillor broadcasts the Prairie Home Companion Show over National Public Radio every Saturday night. Like many Minnesotans, we are solid fans of the show, arming ourselves with a bowl of popcorn and sitting close by the fire in the winter as Garrison's mellow voice fills our cabin with humorous tales from the mythical Minnesota town of Lake Woebegon. For most Minnesotans, satire of the Midwest is an enjoyable serving in our literary diet. Minnesota authors have long explored the life-style of the mid-continent. Northfield's O. E. Rolvaag described the immigrant experience in *Giants in the Earth*. Midwestern provincialism makes an appearance in *Main Street* and Gopher Prairie, a fictionalized Minnesota town modeled after author Sinclair Lewis' Sauk Centre hometown. Saint Paul writer F. Scott Fitzgerald wrote about the poverty of wealth and the complexity of modern life, while Florence Page and Francis Lee Jaques concentrated on Minnesota's physical environment, as did Walter O'Meara and Sigurd Olson.

The freeway from Saint Paul to Minneapolis is getting busy by four in the afternoon, so I find a comfortable speed in the slow lane and we watch with amazement the heavy traffic of commuters moving surely between the Twin Cities. As we near the Mississippi River bridge, a flood of University of Minnesota traffic joins the afternoon migration and we slow to a crawl. Enrolled in academic fields ranging from Aerospace Engineering to Zoology, there are forty thousand registered students at the University, and we are happy that thousands of them use the metropolitan bus system instead of the freeway. The University is comprised of ten colleges, a half dozen schools, including the prestigious law and medical schools, and a number of programs and departments which attract students from all over the world. Another twenty thousand students attend one of eleven, private, four-year colleges in Minneapolis and Saint Paul. The metropolitan area has six community colleges, two private junior colleges, and eight public, vocational-technical institutes. Minnesotans value education. By the time statehood was achieved in 1858, there were already

seventy-two school districts, and within three years 466 schools — about half of them in log cabins. Public education was important to the people on the frontier, especially important to immigrants who wanted to learn to read, write, and speak English.

The freeway, now packed with scholars as well as commuters, is slow going. We recall moments from our University of Minnesota years, moments shared by alumni of all ages at a time of awakening, a time of love and energy, a time as well of frustration and the building strength of purpose. We remember the crisp fall days, homecoming, and the snow falling outside classroom windows while we wrote our finals. Four years seemed an eternity then, more life itself than preparation for a life to come.

When we exit and enter the neighborhood, traffic is as hectic as rush hour on the freeway, but it is moving and we eventually pull into the driveway of a white colonial house on a quiet street which has recently lost several large elm trees to disease. We are met at the door and ushered through the house to the backyard where a gas barbecue is sputtering, and children are playing on a bright blue swing set. While our friends attend to the children, Jeanne and I relax. Many of our city friends were surprised that we moved to the country. Twin Citians go "up north" and "to the lake" on summer weekends, but if someone doesn't come back by Monday, friends become concerned. If you do not come back for four years, friends raise their eyebrows and indulge your waywardness until the day you come to your senses and return.

The reason for the concern is simple: the Twin Cities are a superb place to live. The quality of life is high: the crime rate is low, the air quality is clean; neighborhoods are a pleasant mixture of old and young people with an interest in maintaining a sense of community. People transferred to the Twin Cities are reluctant to leave. In the 1970s, *Time Magazine* featured Minnesota's *Good Life* and credited much of Minnesota's good fortune to a clean German and Scandinavian upbringing.

"We are predictable", it has been said, "and the price we pay for predictability is dullness". Minneapolis and Saint Paul are not New York or Boston. They are not as electric, not as diverse. Harboring exceptional orchestras, including the Minnesota Orchestra and the Saint Paul Chamber Orchestra, theater, art galleries, and museums, the Twin Cities are a chain of neighborhoods tied together in the common belief that the *Good Life* is found in the family, home, school, church, and workplace — and in a walk around a city lake at night without getting mugged.

After dinner our friends invite us to walk around Lake Harriet, along an asphalt pathway beneath oak and cottonwood and an

auroral night sky lit from below by bright city lights. It is easy to become caught in the spell of Twin Cities lake life, easy to be seduced by the tranquility of an inner city park whose quiet prevails over the thunder of the city marketplace. Sailboats are moored and bobbing in a light chop. People are jogging through the darkness and out into streetlight and back again into the black of the lakeshore forest. The voices of happy couples drift across the dark beaches, and the jets that climb high into the Minnesota night seem only tendrils of the metropolitan organism, reaching out for a firm grasp to the country beyond the Midwest.

As we lie abed, wide awake in the twilight of city streetlight, I suggest we drive into farm country in the morning. Jeanne loves the idea and we finally fall asleep listening to the whistle of the fresh fall wind at the window.

THE OTHER MINNESOTA

To some residents, the metropolitan area *is* Minnesota. The roadways which snake into the state's interior are often thought of as paths to a fishing lake, a hunting ground, a quaint restaurant in a river town, or an out-state ski chalet. The interior itself may be threatening to some city residents because it is so big and empty and without any apparent purpose. The other Minnesota is thought to be sprinkled with small, provincial villages, where one might expect to see a farmer standing by his pickup talking with friends. The farmers stare at you as you approach, and then they break up and drift away. The one you manage to capture turns out to be as shy as a four year old. But the Minnesota farmer is a gentleman who knows purpose in the "big empty land". He is a gambler — among the best — who plays his future against the whims of nature. The Minnesota farmer is a businessman in Levis, he is an ecologist, an animal scientist, and a mechanic. Man or woman, the farmer knows the source of the milk we drink, the bacon and the egg we eat. He knows the deep cold of morning in the lambing shed, the frostbite of the January wind, and the baking hot heat of the summer hay. The only thing that terrifies a Minnesota farmer is a city man with a question.

At sunrise we leave the Twin Cities and cross the Mississippi River heading south for Rochester. On the bridge we search the wooded hill to our left for a glimpse of Fort Snelling. After the fort was built, a cluster of squatters and traders and settlers in transit gathered on the surrounding hills. The traders enjoyed the river traffic, the squatters planted corn, and the families of the settlers felt comforted by the soldiers' presence. For twenty years the Army paid little attention to the growing community outside the fort gates. But when the whiskey trade became too brisk, and the squatters began to threaten the fort's

timber supply, the soldiers cleared the area of cabins and tenants. Some of the displaced moved downriver a short distance to form a shanty town which became known as Pig's Eye after a whiskey dealer with an odd squint. A year later, a chapel of logs was built and named Saint Paul.

Nine miles north of Fort Snelling on the Mississippi, at the Falls of Saint Anthony, a sawmill began cutting the logs which came down from the northern pineries, and in 1849 the Village of Saint Anthony was platted. As the Indian lands were ceded to the government, the flood of immigrants followed the Mississippi to Saint Paul, north to winter work in the woods, and west up the Minnesota River to the virgin prairie. In 1855, with a substantial development on the west bank of the Falls, Minneapolis, a Dakota-Greek word meaning "City of Falling Waters", was platted. The "Twins" were launched: Minneapolis with lumber and flour mills; Saint Paul with river traffic and the responsibility of the state capitol.

As we climb away from the Minnesota River Valley and pass through a corridor of light industry, we are suddenly in farmland surrounded by soybeans. From horizon to horizon the sea of cropland awaits harvest under a bright dome of blue sky. There are about fifty-four million acres of land in Minnesota, and about half of that land is under cultivation. Statistically, a farmer in Minnesota manages 295 acres and works 4,390 hours a year to produce enough food for eighty people.

Minnesota produces more sweet corn than any other state — 684 tons of it in 1982, and most of it is grown by farmers under a contract with a state food-processing company. During the corn pick in early August, a visitor may see caravans of harvesting equipment on the back roads of southern Minnesota. Picked at the moment it is fully ripe, the corn is rushed to a processing station for canning and freezing before the rich sugar turns to starch. A lucky Minnesotan knows a farm family who grows sweet corn and gets an invitation to join the family for supper in early August.

We had received such an invitation and arrived at our host's farm one afternoon. I sat with men in the shade of a willow tree where the talk was slow in the heat of the day, but where it was nevertheless talk about soybeans and weather. A farmer lives with his work. There is much mechanization on the modern farm which speeds production. Home computers have helped the farmer organize his office work, agrobiology has helped the farmer develop sound herds and prosperous fields, but in the end it is these men sitting under the willow who must rise before dawn to milk the Holstein and feed the pigs and worry over the rain that will prevent a harvest — or worry over the lack of rain that will prevent a robust crop. No matter how large the farm, or how small, whether it be a family farm or a conglomerate, the farmer, the manager, must play his experience and his education against the force of nature.

The front door opened, and a woman stepped out into the bright sun and yelled, "The water's boiling!" The men roared with delight, jumped from their lawn chairs and piled into a pickup truck. We drove past the farmhouse and down around the barn where we passed through a gate and out into a pasture that led to the field of sweet corn. When we arrived, everyone jumped out of the truck and found large ears of corn which we broke off the stalk and threw into the truck. In a few minutes we had more than fifty, and we all piled in and drove to the farmhouse, shucking corn as we bounced along, to be met in the driveway by women who gathered the golden ears into baskets and rushed them into the boiling water. The reason for all our haste was found in the eating. Accompanied by fresh homemade bread and roast beef, the corn was extra tender and sweet. So sweet that the table talk amounted to pleasurable groans and breathless thank you's. Eventually we all retired to the lawn chairs where, after a few moments of silence, the conversation again turned to the matter of weather and beans. Some of us managed a walk, and I fell in step with our host who started off for the barn at a brisk clip. The day of the diversified farm, the Old MacDonald Farm, was over, said my friend. Today, a farmer has to put his limited resources into a single effort. The barn we were rapidly approaching no longer harbored a dairy herd, it had become an equipment shed—a kind of shop—on a farm which grew peas and sweet corn on contract for a cannery. The farmer lit a cigarette by the gate which led to the pasture. He watched the red sky of evening, as his cigarette smoke, curling above his head, caught the orange light. He said that when he was a boy he used to sit on the fence post here and watch the dairy herd come in from the field.

Fifty miles south of the Twin Cities the land rolls: the fields are smaller, and there is more pastureland than cropland. Here the soil is denser, the forest of oak is thick, and the hills are sprinkled with dairy cattle. We pass recently closed roadside stands whose signs still advertise honey, sweet corn, and homemade jam. Traffic along the route has increased. Trucks and trailers moving north and south flash the names of Minnesota trucking companies: Super Valu, Briggs, Murphy. Soon we leave the freeway for the quiet blacktop road to Wabasha on the Mississippi River.

Driving east we find ourselves winding down through hollows and ravines. Farmhouses perch on roadside terraces, while barns and sheds appear glued to the sides of steep hills which tower above. This is the beginning of the Minnesota that the glaciers missed. But the glacial meltwaters from the north and west cut deep into the sedimentary rock of southeastern Minnesota, as the ancient floodwater worked its way to the Mississippi. What glacial drift may have existed here from an earlier ice sheet has eroded away, leaving rugged, ragged, limestone outcrops high on the steep bluffs.

Midway on our journey to Wabasha we begin to climb out of the valley and reach a high plateau where once again the fields are broad and the dairy cattle walk on level ground. Then the road falls away, and farmhouses perch, and cattle climb, and the town of Wabasha lies just ahead, spread out on the Mississippi floodplain. Far out on the channel, a tug is pushing three loaded barges downstream.

Fifteen million tons of grain, coal, iron, and steel were floated down the Mississippi in 1982. Once the main road into Minnesota, the River, like Lake Superior, became an economical way to move large, heavy, bulky loads. A river barge, about two hundred feet long and forty feet wide, is capable of carrying a load of 1,500 tons with a shallow draft. We walk the muddy shore, as the barge disappears downriver. Finding a high spot we sit for a moment and listen to the River.

The Mississippi has seen it all: the Indians, the French explorers and missionaries, the fur traders and loggers and millers. The river road carried the bark canoes of the Dakota and the trappers and the keel boats of the first American explorers in the early nineteenth century. It floated the log rafts and the flat boats and brought the first steamer, the *Virginia,* to Fort Snelling in 1823. The steamboats carried Minnesota's produce, lumber and grain, downriver and brought thousands of immigrants into the state during the peak years of Mississippi steamboating — 1840 to 1860. The Mississippi steamers quickly evolved from simple shacks tied to a raft of logs to become floating palaces, paddlewheel hotels, bedecked with gay Victorian glitter, glass chandeliers, and polished hardwood railings. The *Grand Republic,* the *Redstone,* the *Quincy,* the *War Eagle,* and *Galena* churned the muddy waters of the Mississippi from New Orleans to Saint Paul. The *Favorite,* the *Anthony Wayne,* the *Nominee,* the *Yankee,* and the *Frank Steele* wound their way up the crooked Minnesota River carrying settlers and tourists who, like Henry David Thoreau, found Minnesota's interior wild and exciting. And, in June of 1861, Mississippi River steamboats carried the First Minnesota Infantry to the Civil War and the battle of Bull Run.

Following the River south to Winona, we hug the high limestone bluffs on our west and look east over the vast floodplain at the waterfowl sanctuaries of the Upper Mississippi River Wildlife and

Fish Refuge. The bottomlands are a tangle of sloughs and bayous and ponds which attract migrating birds like the whistling swan and white pelican. We arrive in Winona hungry, and after a quick lunch drive through the city that was once one of Minnesota's great sawmill towns and later the fourth largest wheat market in the United States. Today, Winona has a population of twenty-five thousand and is home to three colleges and more than one hundred manufacturing firms. We decide to drive west out of the town on an old stretch of highway that parallels a speedy interstate a few miles south. Again we climb the steep bluffs of the Mississippi, this time heading for Rochester, the urban center of southern Minnesota and home of the Mayo Clinic.

More than two hundred thousand people visit the Mayo Clinic every year and they hail from the world over. Farmers and merchants and presidents and kings have all come to the Clinic seeking thorough medical examination and highly specialized attention. Ahead, we see the skyline of the growing city—the buildings of the medical complex and the homes and institutions which have grown with Rochester for the past one hundred and twenty-five years. The rich farmland gives way to development as we enter the city's east side and work our way to the downtown, which is still dominated by nine Mayo buildings and the hospitals and hotels serving the patients and their families.

When William Worrall Mayo began his medical practice in Rochester in 1864, the town had just become a wheat trading center. Grain buyers from Chicago and Milwaukee lined the streets, as farmers brought their wheat to the elevators. Deals were struck, wheat was unloaded, and, money in hand, farm families stocked up on supplies at Rochester businesses. The city's economy boomed, the population grew, and Doc Mayo's practice thrived.

But Mayo's country practice gave him more than the experience of long rides on horseback into the winter countryside to treat homebound farm families. He witnessed the often unfair treatment of farmers by big business, the railroads in particular, and he became a spokesman for the agrarian crusade. In his daily rounds, Mayo found farm families struggling to earn a living at a time when the price for wheat was at its highest. In 1882, the doctor was elected mayor of Rochester and entered the state senate in 1890. As a politician, he was a man for the people, and as a doctor, with his sons William and Charles, he built a medical center for the people. Today, the farmer and the king are served with equal enthusiasm at the Mayo Clinic. Rochester, which has grown to become the fourth largest city in the state with a population of sixty thousand, has made room for manufacturing, most notably International Business Machines, which arrived in 1957.

As the afternoon wanes, we head for overnight accommodations in Northfield, a city forty miles south of Minneapolis and Saint Paul. Driving north out of Rochester, we return to the gentle hills and dairy farms of southern Minnesota. We turn west and shortly cross a set of railroad tracks no longer in service. The abandoned railroad grade is an artifact of the settlement of Minnesota during the late nineteenth century. The railroad was the principal transportation for people and freight during the early 1900s, before the automobile and a network of highways replaced the train as a first choice for personal travel. By 1925, travelers drove over a half million cars, and railway passenger demand was down by half. The train had brought immigrants to their land and it had carried their produce to market. It had tied Minnesota to the rest of the nation and Minnesota's small towns to the metropolitan center. Railroad depots became the focus of small towns whose news arrived as milk was loaded. The railroad was responsible for the economic strength of towns like Northfield.

Not long ago, Northfield called itself the town of "Cows, Colleges and Contentment," but lately it has dropped references to these specifics, preferring to call itself "A Special Place." And it is. Surrounded by some of the richest farmland in Minnesota, home to two excellent private colleges, Northfield people are content to have maintained an attractive city forty miles south of the Twin Cities. The city developed around the Cannon River in the 1850s, growing with the installation of three waterpowered mills, which produced about three thousand barrels of flour a day during the wheat boom of the 1860s and 70s. Today, the population is more than twelve thousand, and many residents commute to work in the Twin Cities.

We drive a few miles east of Northfield to visit friends who own a small airport and farm in the Village of Stanton. It was there, on a broad grass strip, that I learned to fly. What I saw during those first flights was miles and miles of flat field broken only by a few east-west highways and railroad tracks. Rural towns and villages hung close to those tracks like charms on a necklace. It was the rail service and the grain elevators which had created the towns. It was the grocery and the hardware stores, the churches and schools, which anchored the towns when rail service faded away. Southwestern Minnesota was a great ocean of prairie when the settlers arrived. Like a quiet sea, the land rose in swells, and the breezes pressed the tall grass so there was motion, always motion on the prairie through which the settlers' covered wagons, the prairie schooners, moved as ships at sea in search of harbor. There were hundreds of settlers in the 1850s, thousands more in the sixties and seventies. They came in search of the rich, deep, black prairie soil, and soon they would grow wheat, and the railroad

Left to right: A silicon chip exemplifies Minnesota high-tech. ■ The Saint Croix River Dalles. ■ Outdoor sculpture at the Walker Art Museum. ■ Hot air balloons at the Saint Paul Winter Carnival. ■

would come, and the elevators would be built, and the towns would grow around the marketplace.

Today, southwestern Minnesota is a principal food factory in the state for corn and soybeans, beef and hogs. In Willmar stands the world's largest turkey processing plant. On Minnesota's border with Iowa, in the town of Jackson, one can see the first homes of settlers on the treeless prairie: houses built of sod. In Marshall, thirty miles from the South Dakota border, one can visit the Lyon County Historical Museum and see the covered wagon which brought the immigrant and the plow which broke the tough prairie grasses. But it was near present-day Redwood Falls, on the Minnesota River, thirty-five miles east of Marshall, that an event took place which gave all Minnesota a shock.

On Sunday, August 17, 1862, five white settlers were murdered by four Dakota Indians in Meeker County in west-central Minnesota. The next day, the Dakota War began. Two hundred painted warriors attacked the Indian agency near Redwood Falls, killing traders and settlers and looting and burning homesteads. There was panic on the frontier, as the Indians stormed through the district for five weeks. When the United States Army finally crushed the revolt, over five hundred settlers and soldiers were dead, and the farms and homes along the Minnesota River were destroyed. The dreams of opportunity in the fertile valley had been dashed, and the call for revenge was loud and clear. Indians were imprisoned and hung and banished from Minnesota lands. The unrest which had exploded in war was traced to the pressure of settlement on the native lands and to the treaties that the government had made but not maintained with the Indians. Annuities, supplies, food that had been promised failed to show up on schedule and often fell into the hands of unscrupulous traders. The Indians were crowded together on reservations where crop failures led to hunger. A trader advised the agent at the Lower Sioux Agency that if the Indians were hungry he should, "Let them eat grass."

When we leave Northfield and travel for the next few days along the roads that lead deep into western Minnesota, we see prosperous farms and industry where, a hundred and twenty years before, frontier settlers had been jolted by grim realities: mistreated Indians, bitter cold winters, spring blizzards, prairie and forest fires, drought, and flood. The land, these settlers would learn, was exhaustible. The wheat would rust, the soil would erode, the forests would burn in a conflagration which would destroy entire towns. Survival would mean learning how to use the tools of conservation. Old country know-how would be replaced by courses from the University of Minnesota in plant pathology, soil chemistry, and animal science. Forestland would be replanted, and the Indians would be educated — and pushed into living apart from the white man and his new country.

We drive across the flatlands of northwestern Minnesota, the lake bed of Glacial Lake Agassiz. It is a land of wheat and barley, of oats and sugar beets, and it is a land of light industry: snowmobiles are manufactured in Roseau, near the Minnesota border with Canada; hockey sticks are produced in Warroad, Roseau's eastern neighbor. These are the cities on the western reaches of the "voyageur's highway", three hundred miles northwest of Minneapolis and Saint Paul. "We believe in hard work up here", a Warroad friend told me. "There is no substitute for it, and it wouldn't be much of a life up here without it." A hundred miles south of Warroad, in the lake district, the economy is also dependent upon hard work — and tourists.

Like agriculture, tourism in Minnesota is a staple of the economic diet: about one hundred thousand full-time jobs are dependent upon the tourist trade. As Minnesota's Office of Tourism reaches out to attract more visitors, it overcomes the stereotype of the state as a cold, remote outpost and encourages year-round use of the state's lakes, ski trails, and forests.

The lakes are beautiful and quiet as we drive through the resort country on a brisk fall morning. The cabin owners are closing their buildings for winter, while many resorts are preparing for snowmobilers, ice fishermen, and skiers. There is a wholesome, positive feeling among businessmen in this recreational country, in spite of high costs, rugged competition, and a few slow months during the year. Resort owners seem satisfied that the tourists will soon be using the state's resources all four seasons.

Gradually we turn northeast for the north shore and the Boundary Waters Canoe Area. We stop when we get to the iron range. Residents here, who call themselves The Rangers, are the iron miners of Minnesota. They live in the cities of northeastern Minnesota, where iron ore was discovered in the middle of the nineteenth century. Today, the mines are primarily tourist attractions — holes several miles-long, a mile wide, and hundreds of feet deep. In the 1930s, these open-pit mines provided nearly two-thirds of all the iron taken from the earth in the United States. It was the iron which built the cities on the iron mining district and attracted thousands of immigrants. A century of iron mining created thousands of miles of railroad track from the mines to the harbor at Duluth. The harbor expanded; the Saint Lawrence River Seaway opened Minnesota's iron to the markets of the world and

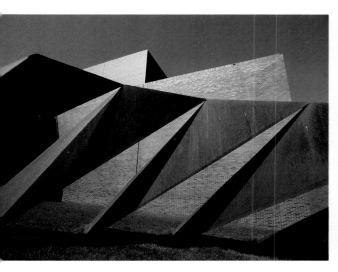

brought foreign competition to markets in the Midwest.

It all began just after the Civil War, when a gold strike brought prospectors to the shores of Vermillion Lake in the pristine north country. There was little gold, but the man who had helped to build Duluth, the entrepreneur Jay Cooke, urged the mining of the iron which lay just beneath the surface of rock and soil. Cooke encouraged smelting, but the wealth would come from the shipping of ore to the blast furnaces in Cleveland and Pittsburgh.

In the fall of 1892 the first ore traveled by rail to the harbor. Ore docks were constructed, and in 1893 John D. Rockefeller formed the Lake Superior Consolidated Iron Mines Company. By 1900, six million tons of ore were being shipped annually to the mills on the Great Lakes. In 1901 the United States Steel Corporation was formed and along with a subsidiary, the Oliver Mining Company, controlled most of the mines in the Mesabi Range. The shipments of ore grew to thirty-eight million tons in 1916, and during World War I the demand was so high that two hundred thousand tons were loaded in a single day. Railway carloads of ore moved from the mines to the harbor, miners were hired, homes, schools, churches—whole cities—built. They said it would never end. In 1929 fifty million tons of ore were shipped to the mills.

Then came the Great Depression—the Crash. The mills closed, the mines closed, and the harbor fell quiet. The shock rolled through the Range leaving ghost towns in its wake. World War II created new demand, the towns were resettled, and again the ore moved to the docks in Duluth. In the 1950s, when the United States became the world's greatest producer of steel, Minnesota's mines produced the ore.

Prosperity returned to the Range for a time, and then the resource began to disappear. Hematite, the high-grade ore of the Mesabi, had been mined to near depletion. The development of the taconite industry has shored up the economy, but the recession of the 1980s, the closing of mills, and the decreasing demand for steel products have once again created dramatic unemployment. The residents, however, are tough — very tough. The Rangers have learned to hang on, to wait for the day when the demand for taconite will return. They are survivors.

As we drive away from the Range cities, we leave with images of homes for sale, cars and trucks and bikes for sale, businesses boarded up, streets empty of people. The State of Minnesota is searching for alternative job opportunities in northeastern Minnesota and studying the possibility of peat mining. Peat may prove a cost-effective energy resource and the beginning of new life on the Range. Peat production may simply be a gesture of the hope that Minnesotans have that the land will always provide jobs.

As we drive through Duluth and start our one hundred and fifty-mile journey up the North Shore, we see others who have chosen to vacation in the boundary waters in fall. Cars pass us with canoes tied to their tops and sleeping bags stuffed in back seat windows. In summer the North Shore Drive is packed with tourists in short sleeves. Today the traffic is light and swift and few pause to watch Lake Superior lash at the granite boulders on the shore. The herring gulls are soaring into the brisk wind, and far out on the horizon we see a lone Lake freighter sailing toward Duluth.

At Grand Marais, on the northeastern tip of Minnesota's shore, we quickly stock up with food and fuel and begin an hour's drive into the wilderness surrounding the Gunflint Trail. We talk about the Minnesota that we have seen, about the people who have built the state, and about those who are working now to maintain a balance between the economic goals and the pristine character of the land. The history of Minnesota is in part a history of resource exploitation. The beaver, the white pine, the prairie, and the ores have each in their time been consumed to fuel growth and to create wealth and employment. Today, Minnesotans want to preserve as well as to consume.

Later, we canoe through the fog of early morning on a lake near the Canadian border. We paddle slowly to listen for the call of the loon and to let the lake capture us. The mist is so thick that we feel an imbalance, and suddenly we seem to be moving faster and faster into the veil and into the morning gray of the forest around us. But we have not moved, and I have just dipped my paddle into the still water when the loon calls. We drift in the silence that is broken and suddenly we feel for all the world that this is the last resource, this is the last lake, and it must never be taken for what it is worth today, but spared for what it is worth to all time.

Right: A pair of common loons on Lake Two in the Boundary Waters. A large aquatic bird, the loon is an excellent swimmer and diver and has come to symbolize the wilderness of northern Minnesota because of its independence and its preference for remote and isolated lakes.

Left: Cherokee Lake, the Boundary Waters. The crystalline character of Minnesota's wilderness lakes has not changed significantly since the late eighteenth and early nineteenth centuries, when French-Canadian voyageurs traveled these waters in search of fur. *Below:* Snow-covered mounds of sphagnum moss in a northern Minnesota peat bog. Bog land is extensive and Minnesota officials are exploring the feasibility of peat production.

Below: Black spruce, birch, maple, and aspen make up a large part of the North Shore forest canopy. Before loggers arrived during the late nineteenth century, white pine, Norway and jack pine, and balsam fir were the upland's principal trees. *Right:* More moose are killed during hunting season in Minnesota than in any other state but Alaska. Each year thousands of hunters bag hundreds of moose, the state's largest game animal, each weighing six hundred to nine hundred pounds.

Left: An Indian powwow in Grand Portage on the northeastern tip of Minnesota. The Ojibway Indians helped to make Grand Portage one of the most important fur-trading centers in North America during the late 1700s. *Below:* Lake Superior is the largest of the Great Lakes and the second-largest body of fresh water in the world. The lake has witnessed violent storms which have taken a heavy toll in ships and sailors since the days of the voyageurs more than three hundred years ago. *Overleaf:* Winter comes early to the forests of the north country. A snowstorm in September or October is not unusual.

Below: The observant visitor may spot a black bear like this cub on the North Shore browsing the roadsides for berries and insects. The state's black bear population is estimated to be in the range of eight to ten thousand animals. *Right:* Numbering close to a million, the whitetail deer is Minnesota's most popular and abundant large game animal. Although more than four hundred thousand hunters take to the woods each November, the deer population remains high.

Left: Fall flooding swells Slim Creek near the Boundary Waters in northern Saint Louis County. Streams and rivers on the northern slope flow to the Canadian border and from there to Hudson Bay. *Below:* Over fifteen hundred resorts, in picturesque and rustic locations, serve over twenty-five million vacationers in Minnesota year-round.

Below: Bog cotton, or cotton grass, tossing in the wind near Zim in northeastern Minnesota. The high acid content of a bog's groundwater encourages the growth of many unique and specialized plants. *Right:* Nearly a half century ago, men and machines digging out the world's richest supply of iron ore filled these canyons. A forest of birch and aspen has reclaimed this abandoned open-pit mine near Hibbing.

Left: Rising from a group of large lakes in the Boundary Waters, the Temperance River flows south twenty-five miles, cascading through deep canyons and thundering through the gorges of the Temperance River State Park, before it empties into Lake Superior. *Below:* Weighing only a few ounces, the saw-whet owl is the smallest owl found in Minnesota. It is a surprisingly tame bird whose voice sounds like the filing of a saw. Saw-whets usually nest in tree cavities created by woodpeckers.

Below: The work of a beaver on a northern Minnesota aspen tree. Trapped nearly to extinction during the middle of the nineteenth century, the beaver has made a strong comeback on lakes and streams flanked by birch and aspen forests. *Right:* Bear River in the George Washington State Forest, north of Grand Rapids, offers fisherman, camper, and hiker the unspoiled, wild beauty of the Minnesota North Woods.

Left: Sunrise on Rainy Lake in the Voyageurs National Park on Minnesota's border with Canada. Once a segment of the Voyageurs Highway across North America, this national park includes one hundred and sixty thousand acres of land and water.
Below: This weather-worn structure, a monument to the days when the North Shore was alive with loggers and commercial fishermen, stands in decay in a sea of fireweed. Today, towns along the North Shore cater to a brisk tourist trade.

Below: Cross-country skiing, a popular sport with Minnesotans, is made even more enticing by the wilderness setting. The Minnesota Department of Natural Resources maintains more than a thousand miles of groomed ski trails in state parks and forests. *Right:* The timber wolf, loved by some because it represents the rugged wilderness, is despised by others who believe that it preys upon livestock and whitetail deer. It is estimated that there are twelve hundred timber wolves in residence in the state — second only to Alaska. *Overleaf:* Fall color runs wild in the understory of a Norway pine plantation on the Nett Lake Indian Reservation, south of International Falls. Norway, or red pine, is Minnesota's state tree.

Left: Wind power pumped the water on this northwestern Minnesota farm not far from the Old Crossing Treaty State Wayside where, in 1863, the United States received five million acres of fertile lands from the Ojibway Indians. *Below:* Fall leaves carpet the ground twenty miles north of Park Rapids. Attracting thousands of tourists each year who come to see the source of the Mississippi River, Itasca is the state's largest and most developed park.

Below: Wheat harvest in the Red River Valley. Once a part of the buffalo's summer feeding range, the Red River Valley is less a valley than a broad, vast, flat plain etched by the rivers and streams of northwestern Minnesota. *Right:* Combining wheat near Hallock in the far northwestern corner of Minnesota. During the mid-nineteenth century, settlers planted wheat so intensively that the soil was robbed of nutrients, and farmers soon practiced the economy of crop rotation.

Left: Otter Tail County is a region rich in sky blue water and wooded hills. The Otter Tail River flows through the county seat, Fergus Falls, where hydroelectric power is generated for much of the western part of the state. *Below:* The lake region of central Minnesota is home to many of Minnesota's larger resorts.

Below: Waiting for the school bus during an early morning in March. Minnesota's school-bus fleet travels over a half million miles a day in all but the worst snow conditions to carry the more than seven hundred thousand children enrolled in the state's public schools. *Right:* Although Minnesota enjoys four distinct seasons, winter is most vivid when the state is under the influence of cold polar winds and snow.

Left: Pressure ridge of ice on Lake Lida, east of Pelican Rapids. Lakes in the central region of the state are popular with fishermen seeking to catch walleye, northern pike, and a variety of panfish. *Below:* The Mississippi River headwaters rise out of the wetlands of Lake Itasca in northern Minnesota wilderness and travel 2,350 miles to the Gulf of Mexico.

Below: A shelterbelt of trees planted to break the force of wind across the plains of the northwestern counties. Windbreaks help to stabilize the very fine, sandy soils on what was once the bed of Glacial Lake Agassiz, an ice-age body of water that covered all of northwestern Minnesota. *Right:* Rows of grain climb into the morning light on a farm in Marshall County.

Left: Norwegian settlers brought excellent farming skills, and their religion, to the Red River Valley during the years following the Civil War. *Below:* A spring snowstorm near Halstead in the Red River Valley. Once wheat country, the Valley today produces flax, barley, sugar beets, potatoes, and new varieties of soybeans able to withstand a short growing season. *Overleaf:* Aspen and a scattering of pine tell the story of the logging industry which began in the Lake Itasca region during the late 1850s.

Below: Summer storm clouds roll low over lush southern Minnesota farmland, bringing moisture and breaking heat spells. *Right:* Prairie grass lies flat in a dawn frost in Blue Mounds State Park in the southwest corner of the state. Rock County is the only county in Minnesota which has no natural lake. *Overleaf:* Anglers gather on a highway bridge over Lac Qui Parle Lake on the Minnesota River in Chippewa County. In 1930, a mud catfish weighing 157 pounds was caught in the River.

Left: Pasqueflowers open with the morning sun on the Nature Conservancy's 222-acre Hole-in-the-Mountain prairie near Lake Benton. There were 18 million acres of prairie in the state before settlers broke the land with their plows. Today, only seventy-five thousand acres of relatively intact prairie remain. *Below:* A black-crowned night heron feeds in Marsh Lake Wildlife Refuge near Odessa on the Minnesota River.

Below: There is no dieting for this porker on an Albert Lea farm in Freeborn County. Minnesota ranks third in hog production in the country. *Right:* Glaciers deposited as much as one hundred and fifty feet of rich soil over what is now Blue Earth County in southern Minnesota. Once home to buffalo, county lands include some of the finest farmland in the state.

Left: Granite quarry near Ortonville, a city on the state's western border with South Dakota. The red, or mahogany colored, stone taken from quarries in western Big Stone County is used for facing-material on buildings and for monuments and memorials. *Below:* Twenty miles south of Ortonville, near Madison, Minnesota, cowboys herd a few beef cattle to pasture. The state ranks tenth in the nation in beef production.

Below: Butterfield Antique Steam and Gas Engine Threshing Festival, Watonwan County. Minnesotans love their community celebrations, whether it is the Korn and Klover Karnival in Hinckley in the north, or the King Turkey Days in the south. *Right:* Fall comes to Browns Valley on the Continental Divide in western Minnesota. From this border town, the Red River flows north and the Minnesota River begins its journey south.

Left: The Alexander Ramsey Falls in Redwood Falls City Park, where the Redwood River rushes through the Minnesota River Valley, seem almost out of character for the southwest prairie. *Below:* Soybean flower in Stevens County near Morris. The state ranks in the country's top five in soybean production. *Overleaf:* There is no time to lose when the feed corn is ready to harvest. Crews work long hours in the fall to deliver the summer's crop to elevators in towns across the state.

Below: A farm on the highland above the Cannon River Valley near Welch in Goodhue County. The Dakota Indians gave up this land by treaty in 1851, and settlers began to farm the area several years later. *Right:* A limestone outcrop catches the first light of day on a Money Creek Valley farm in the far southeastern county of Houston. Early Norwegian settlers found familiar terrain in this unglaciated region of the state.

Left: An apple harvest in southeastern Minnesota today is due, in part, to Peter Gideon, an Ohio native who brought apple seedlings into the state in 1850. Gideon, after years of struggle, produced a hybrid, the Wealthy, which was hardy enough to survive Minnesota winters. *Below:* The end of a long day on a Spring Valley farm in Fillmore County. Once caught up in the wheat frenzy of the late 1800s, many southern Minnesota farms today are primarily dairy operations.

Below: The Winnebago Creek in the southeastern county of Houston flows into the Mississippi River after winding through pastureland beneath limestone bluffs in the "driftless area," the only region in Minnesota untouched by glaciers. *Right:* From the broad, flat plateau of farmland above the Mississippi River, the road suddenly dives down steep slopes in a series of switchbacks to reach the Mississippi River Valley floor below.

Left: Boathouses on the Mississippi River in Red Wing, the Good-hue County seat. A popular stopping place for steamboats in the 1850s, Red Wing has restored many of its nineteenth century buildings and homes and renewed the flavor of a Minnesota river town. *Below:* Canadian geese hug the rolling wooded hills of the Whitewater River Valley on their way to nearby fields to feed.

Below: Barge traffic moves downriver on the Mississippi above Winona. Here the River is part of the Upper Mississippi Wildlife and Fish Refuge, from Wabasha, Minnesota to Rock Island, Illinois — a distance of three hundred miles, where two hundred thousand acres of fishing, camping, hiking, boating, and hunting are preserved for the public. *Right:* The city lights of Rochester reflect on Silver Lake, a one-time millpond where thousands of geese winter in waters warmed by the city's powerplant. Rochester is home of the famed Mayo Clinic, where thousands of patients, rich and poor, are treated each year.

Left: Maidenhair fern and wild geranium grow lush in the Beaver Creek Valley State Park in Houston County. Surrounded by limestone bluffs, the park includes a spring brook popular with fishermen in search of a brown trout. *Below:* Red cedar on Coyote Point in Whitewater State Park. It was in the Whitewater Valley in the 1930s that Richard J. Dorer found severe soil erosion and denuded slopes caused by careless farming and logging methods. Dorer fought for woodland restoration, and is today memorialized by a forest bearing his name.

Below: A new entry in Minnesota's system of sixty-four state parks, O. L. Kipp, a mile north of La Crescent along the Mississippi, offers a spectacular view of the River Valley. *Right:* Bright sumac and oak trees live close to industrial activity on the Mississippi River south of Saint Paul. Minnesotans are learning not to trade natural resources carelessly for short-term economic gains. *Overleaf:* A wet October snow sticks fast to maple trees in a forest near Mille Lacs Lake in central Minnesota.

Left: Minnehaha Creek tumbles over the falls during winter in Minnehaha Park. Minneapolis and Saint Paul residents use their inner city park systems to skate, ski, and snowshoe during the long winter months. *Below:* Lights from a Saint Paul home glow warm during an early snowstorm. Twin City residents enjoy the four seasons, and they accept winter's forty-inch snowfall, below zero temperatures, and long winter nights stoically, with a crackling fire and thoughts of spring.

Below: The Minneapolis Institute of Arts is home to a collection of work which represents nearly every period and school of art. Works of Rembrandt and Goya, Chinese bronzes, Japanese prints, photography, decorative arts, and sculpture are on display in the permanent collection, while special exhibits are always on view to more than one quarter of a million visitors annually. *Right:* For most residents the beauty of winter in Minnesota outweighs its severity. Here, under frost-covered maple trees, the cross-country skier takes pleasure when he or she looks up during the season.

Left: Minnesota Dance Theatre members practice in the company's Minneapolis facilities. Twin Citians have shown a strong and enduring interest in the performing arts, supporting nearly one hundred organizations representing dance, theater, opera, concerts, orchestras, and the vocal arts. *Below:* The capitol dome in Saint Paul glows in the twilight, flanked by the Saint Paul Cathedral, a descendant of the log cabin chapel, built in 1841, which gave its name to the city.

Below: With more than eight thousand acres of public land dedicated to recreational use, Minneapolis and Saint Paul are cities of parks. Although the Twin Cities have twenty-five lakes within their limits, residents can choose among nearly six hundred lakes for fishing, boating, or swimming in the seven-county metropolitan area. *Right:* The Minnesota Orchestra performs in Orchestra Hall, Minneapolis. It is hailed as one of the finest halls in the nation, which befits one of the nation's finest orchestras.

Left: A mallard female standing on the shore of a Minneapolis lake where hundreds of ducks gather to feed during the summer. Ducks will remain in the Twin City area during the winter months as long as they can find open water and food. *Below:* A church on the high bluffs overlooking the Dalles of the Saint Croix. The town was settled during the 1850s as the logging industry expanded. Today, largely dependent upon tourist trade, Taylors Falls is home to historic buildings and spectacular views.

Below: Finnish festival dancers perform during one of many ethnic celebrations in the Twin Cities throughout the summer. Visitors may sample foods, buy crafts, and view costumes and dances of the homeland. *Right:* The white pine legacy seems adrift in a bank of fog in the Saint Croix Valley. The state's largest sawmills at Stillwater and Marine cut millions of feet of white pine lumber each year during the nineteenth century.

Left: Fall arrives on a maple woodlot near Shafer in Chisago County. When Swedish immigrants arrived here during the 1850s, land speculation briskly capitalized on the white pine stands which would soon fall. Today, the white pine is gone, and a second growth of hardwood covers the rolling hills which are not being farmed. *Below:* A tiger in the Minnesota Zoo waits for its afternoon feeding. Zoo animals are kept in nearly natural environments. The 480-acre Zoo can be explored on foot, on skis in winter, or in an all-weather monorail. *Overleaf:* The Hubert H. Humphrey Metrodome joined the Minneapolis skyline in 1981.

Below: The cheerful colors of a Saint Paul restoration can be seen in many of the capitol city's neighborhoods and business districts. Saint Paul is a national leader in the preservation of aging and historic buildings. An arts center with galleries, office, and performance space blossomed in the former Federal Courts Building, and a dying warehouse district has become a new urban village in Lowertown. *Right:* An early snow paints a bright fall field east of Saint Paul on river bluffs near Battle Creek Regional Park.

Left: In 1886, Saint Paul built an ice palace and, after a few years delay, began a tradition of winter carnivals, including winter sports, parades, ice sculpture contests, and even water-skiing, when a patch of open water was found. *Below:* Speed skaters wait for the gun on the Como Lake speed skating rink. Minnesotans have long enjoyed winter sports. In 1883, Norwegians started a skiing club in Red Wing; skating and sledding parties were as much a part of rural winter life as were the long hours spent in the forest and at the woodpile behind the barn.

Below: Canoes await customers on Lake Harriet, one of eleven lakes within the Minneapolis park system. A summer's evening may be spent in front of the bandstand for a lakeside concert or on a stroll to take in the rose garden and bird sanctuary. *Right:* Once dependent upon Mississippi River traffic alone, St. Paul today is growing rapidly to meet the economic and social needs of the future.

AFTERWORD

My love for photography and Minnesota began the same summer. As we followed my father to his various Air Force assignments around the country, my family never stopped in Minnesota long enough to get acquainted with the state. Then, one summer between college terms, while working for a camp, I met the wilds of Minnesota's canoe country. Beneath those summer moons began a love which runs deeper and broader than ever. That summer, Minnesota with her moods and her magic slipped a ring upon my finger.

More than a decade has passed since that first summer, and during the past three years while exploring nearly thirty-eight thousand miles of Minnesota's highways, mainstreets, backroads, trails, and waterways to create MINNESOTA II's photographs, the ring gained in lustre, and at certain times, it positively glowed with the colors of a Minnesota harvest moon, the dawn mists of Burntside Lake, the cheeks of tobogganing children.

There is a spirit abounding within Minnesota which lives inside her people. I cannot acknowledge all of you who went out of your way to be friendly and to assist me with this project, but know that your spirits are in these pages. To the following I am deeply indebted: the Minnesota Orchestra, the Minnesota Dance Theatre, the Minneapolis Institute for the Arts, the Minnesota Vikings, Hanna Mining, Control Data, and the Grand Portage Ojibway Tribe for permission to photograph their organizations and people; to the personnel of the Minnesota Historical Society, Minnesota Tourism Department, and the Minnesota State Parks for their special knowledge of events and places; to the State High School Hockey League, Cargill, Aamodt's Orchards, Estrem Farms, Bill Gessner, David Uher, Joe Kellogg, and *Canoe* magazine for providing opportunities to make special images; to Chuck Shubat and Dick George for their superb abilities as pilots; and to Sandy May and Barb Shumsker for their guidance and assistance in editing a mountain of pictures.

Although there is room for only one person behind the camera, the love, support, and encouragement of the following persons made me feel I was never alone: Sheila Arimond, Tom and Liz Heywood, Richard and Jeanne Coffey, Will and Carolyn Smith, Wally and Gloria Nippolt, Peggy Olsson, the Bliss Family, Fran Watson, and Shuby. Special thanks go to Rita Plourde, Kurt Mitchell, Melitta Wainio, and B. Sterling Casselton.

My greatest appreciation is for the infinite patience, understanding and love of my friend, lover, and spouse, JB.

Richard Hamilton Smith